Dedications:

This tribute to my city is dedicated to the memory of my great-grandfather, James Lee, who came to Seattle in 1888, and established Lee's Pharmacy after The Great Seattle Fire in 1889 (This advertisement was placed during the Klondike Gold Rush);

to his wife, Elizabeth Paddock Lee, whose family came west in the mid-1800s, nearly 250 years after landing at Plymouth Rock;

to their daughter (my grandmother), Edith Lee Bragg, born in Seattle in 1900, who graduated from Broadway High School in 1918, and the University of Washington in 1922;

and to her son (my father), Robert Tully Bragg, who, though he was born in Portland, had the good sense to return the family to Seattle 35 years ago.

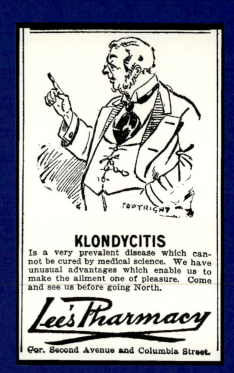

SEATTLE,
City By The Sound

by: L. E. Bragg

photography by: Doug Wilson

This is a statue of Chief Sealth, for whom this city is named.

This is the square where the city began,
home to a statue of Chief Sealth,
for whom this city is named.

These are the
tall buildings
that tower
over the square
where the city began,
home to a statue
of Chief Sealth,
for whom this city is named.

This is the market
between the tall buildings
that tower
over the square where
the city began,
home to a statue
of Chief Sealth,
for whom this city is named.

This is the Space Needle that pierces the sky
above the market,
between the tall buildings that tower
over the square where the city began,
home to a statue of Chief Sealth,
for whom this city is named.

These are the houseboats that float on the lake

beneath the Space Needle
that pierces the sky
above the market,
between the tall
buildings that tower
over the square where the
city began,
home to a statue
of Chief Sealth,
for whom this city is named.

These are the boats that sail through the locks
from the lake where the houseboats float
beneath the Space Needle that pierces the sky
above the market,
between the tall buildings that tower
over the square where the city began,
home to a statue of Chief Sealth,
for whom this city is named.

This is the sound whose waters surround

    the boats that sail through the locks
from the lake
where the houseboats float
beneath the Space Needle that pierces the sky
above the market,
between the tall buildings that tower
over the square where the city began,
home to a statue of Chief Sealth,
for whom this city is named.

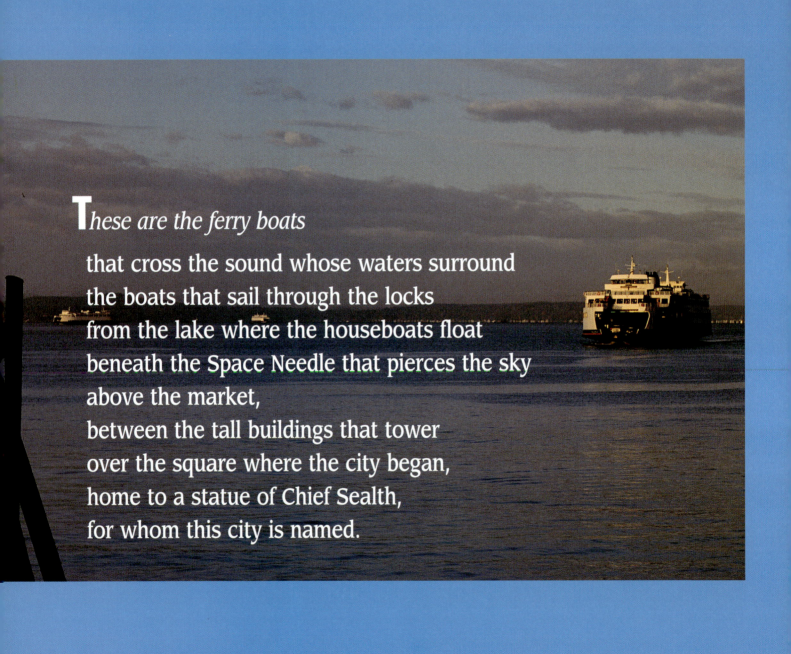

These are the ferry boats

that cross the sound whose waters surround
the boats that sail through the locks
from the lake where the houseboats float
beneath the Space Needle that pierces the sky
above the market,
between the tall buildings that tower
over the square where the city began,
home to a statue of Chief Sealth,
for whom this city is named.

This is the bridge that spans the lands,

   taking people to the ferry boats
   that cross the sound whose waters surround
   the boats that sail through the locks
   from the lake where the houseboats float
   beneath the Space Needle that pierces the sky
   above the market,
   between the tall buildings that tower
   over the square where the city began,
   home to a statue of Chief Sealth,
   for whom this city is named.

This is the lake
that floats
the bridge
that spans
the lands,
taking people
to the
ferry boats
that cross the
sound whose
waters surround the boats that sail through the locks
from the lake where the houseboats float
beneath the Space Needle that pierces the sky
above the market,
between the tall buildings that tower
over the square where the city began,
home to a statue of Chief Sealth,
for whom this city is named.

This is the range where the sun comes up,
and shines on the lake
that floats the bridge that spans the lands,
taking people to the ferry boats
that cross the sound whose waters surround
the boats that sail through the locks

from the lake where the houseboats float
beneath the Space Needle that pierces the sky
above the market,
between the tall buildings that tower
over the square where the city began,
home to a statue of Chief Sealth,
for whom this city is named.

These are the mountains on which the sun sets,
across from the range where the sun comes up,
and shines on the lake
that floats the bridge that spans the lands,
taking people to the ferry boats
that cross the sound whose waters surround
the boats that sail through the locks
from the lake where the houseboats float
beneath the Space Needle that pierces the sky
above the market,
between the tall buildings that tower
over the square where the city began,
home to a statue of Chief Sealth,
for whom this city is named.

Special Thanks to: Karen Larsen, Ph.D.,
"Miss Grammar," for editing;
to Merle Dowd for his publishing advice;
and, to my husband,
David Marich, for his support.

East Seattle Publishing Co.
P.O. Box 761
Mercer Island, Washington 98040

Text copyright
© 1997 by Lynn E. Bragg

Photographic copyright
© 1997 Doug Wilson
(425) 822-8604
All photographs
except those listed below

Photographic copyright
© 1997 David Marich
Market Sign p.10;
Mercer Island Bridge p. 22-23

Photographic copyright
© 1997 L.E. Bragg
Houseboats p. 14-15;
Puget Sound p. 18;
Montlake Cut p. 25

All rights reserved. No part of this book
may be reproduced or transmitted in any
form or by any means, electronic or
mechanical, including photocopying,
recording, or by any information storage
or retrieval system, without the written
permission of East Seattle Publishing Co.,
except where permitted by law.

Design: Susan Bard
Portland, Oregon

Library of Congress Catalog Card Number:
97-60333

ISBN #0-9656755-0-5

Printed by:
C & C Offset Printing Co., Ltd.,
Hong Kong